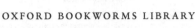

OXFORD BOOKWORMS LIBRARY
*True Story*

# Twelve Years a Slave

SOLOMON NORTHUP

Level 2 (700 headwords)

T0344584

Retold by Clare West
Illustrated by Rebecca Lisotta

Series Editor: Rachel Bladon
Founder Editors: Jennifer Bassett
and Tricia Hedge

# OXFORD
### UNIVERSITY PRESS

Great Clarendon Street, Oxford, OX2 6DP, United Kingdom

Oxford University Press is a department of the University of Oxford.
It furthers the University's objective of excellence in research, scholarship,
and education by publishing worldwide. Oxford is a registered trade
mark of Oxford University Press in the UK and in certain other countries

ISBN: 978 0 19 402411 2

A complete recording of this Bookworms
edition of *Twelve Years a Slave* is available.

Printed and bound in Great Britain by Bell & Bain Ltd, Glasgow

Word count (main text): 9,252

For more information on the Oxford Bookworms Library,
visit www.oup.com/elt/gradedreaders

### ACKNOWLEDGEMENTS

*Cover photographs reproduced with permission from*: Getty Images; (breaking
chains/JDawnInk), Shutterstock; (cotton field/Megan Betteridge).

*The Publisher would like to thank the following for permissions to reproduce
photographs*: Getty Images p.66 (Bookworms Cover: Huckleberry Finn/
Camerique/Hulton Archive), (Factfile cover: Martin Luther King/Hulton
Archive); Shutterstock pp.54 (slaves at work/Mondadori Portfolio),
55 (Abraham Lincoln and men/Everett Historical), 64 (Frederick Douglass/
Everett Historical).

*Illustrations by*: Rebecca Lisotta/Milan Illustrations

# CONTENTS

# UNITED STATES OF AMERICA, 1841

SLAVE STATES

FREE STATES

MAINE

NEW HAMPSHIRE

VERMONT

MASSACHUSETTS

Saratoga

RHODE ISLAND

NEW YORK

CONNECTICUT

New York City

PENNSYLVANIA

NEW JERSEY

DELAWARE

MICHIGAN

Washington

MARYLAND

Richmond

OHIO

VIRGINIA

INDIANA

NORTH CAROLINA

ILLINOIS

KENTUCKY

SOUTH CAROLINA

TENNESSEE

MISSOURI

GEORGIA

ARKANSAS

ALABAMA

MISSISSIPPI

FLORIDA TERRITORY

Red River

Marksville

Indian Creek

New Orleans

Bayou Boeuf

REPUBLIC OF TEXAS

LOUISIANA

N

# INTRODUCTION

In 1841, when this story begins, some people in the United States of America (USA) had slaves. Nearly all these slaves were black. In most of the states in the north, slavery was against the law; these states were called *free states*. In most of the states in the south, slavery was not against the law; these were called *slave states*. A *free man* was a man who was not born a slave. If he traveled to the slave states, and he was black, he needed to carry *free papers*. When people saw these papers, they knew that he was not a slave.

# PEOPLE IN THE STORY

**Solomon Northup**
**Anne Northup**  Solomon's wife
**Mr. Parker**  Solomon's friend
**Mr. Brown and Mr. Hamilton**  circus workers
**James Burch**  a slave-trader
**Eliza**  a slave
**Randall**  Eliza's son
**Emily**  Eliza's daughter
**Theophilus Freeman**  another slave-trader
**William Ford**  Solomon's first master
**Mrs. Ford**  Ford's wife
**John Tibeats**  Solomon's second master
**Mr. Chapin**  Ford's farm manager
**Edwin Epps**  Solomon's third master
**Armsby**  a worker on Epps's farm
**Patsey**  Epps's slave
**Bass**  another worker
**Henry Northup**  Solomon's family friend, a lawyer

## Chapter One
# KIDNAP!

I am going to tell you a story – a story of kidnap, cruelty, and danger. It is a terrible story, and it happened to me. Every word of it is true.

My name is Solomon Northup. But that was not always the name of my family. My father was a slave, and he belonged to the Northup family. When old Mr. Northup died, his family made my father a free man. My father took the Northup family name, because he became free when he was working for them. So he lived as a free man for more than twenty years, until his death in 1829, and I was born a free man, not a slave. By 1841, when my story starts, I was living in Saratoga, a small town in New York State, with my wife Anne and our three children.

Anne worked as a cook at some of the big hotels near our home, and I did some building and farm work, and cut wood. My wife and I had to work hard, but we were happy. When I had any free time, I loved walking with my beautiful children, and I often stopped to talk with my friend Mr. Parker, who had a large store in town.

At home, I liked to play my violin. As a child, and as an adult, too, I was always happiest when I was playing music. Since those days in Saratoga, my violin has helped me through some of the darkest times of my life.

Until that year, 1841, there was nothing unusual about the story of my life. These were just the hopes and loves and hard days of a black man who was trying to make his way in the world. I did not know then that a dark cloud was coming nearer and nearer.

One day in 1841, I said goodbye to my family for a few days. Anne had a job in a hotel twenty miles away, and was taking the children with her.

*I said goodbye to my family for a few days.*

"I'll see you all on Saturday!" I called to them when they left the house.

I was not very busy at that time, so I went into town to look for some work. I was walking down the street when a man called my name.

"Mr. Northup! Could we speak to you, please?"

I turned around at once, and saw two white men, wearing fine clothes, like men from the city. We began talking together. The men worked for a circus, and their names were Brown and Hamilton.

"The circus is in Washington right now," said Brown. "We're on our way there. But first, we have to do some small circus shows in New York City."

"We hear that you're a good violin player," said his friend. "We need some music for our shows. Will you come and play for us?"

"We'll pay you twenty dollars," said Brown, "but we must leave at once."

Twenty dollars! That was a lot of money to me. And I really wanted to see New York City. So I agreed.

We shook hands, and I went home to get my violin and some clothes for the journey. I did not write and tell Anne, because I thought that I would be home soon.

We traveled from Saratoga to New York City. Brown and Hamilton were very kind to me. We stayed in good hotels and ate in good restaurants, and I did not have to pay for anything. I only had to play my violin once. But when we arrived in New York City, Hamilton said, "Our plans have changed, Mr. Northup. We have to hurry on to Washington. Come with us!"

I was not sure at first, but Brown and Hamilton talked excitedly about Washington, and said that I would earn lots of money, so at last I agreed.

"My friend," Brown said, "perhaps you need to get some free papers from the office here in New York City. Slavery is not against the law in Washington, remember. If you have free papers, people will know that you are not a slave."

"Thank you for thinking of that, Mr. Brown," I said, and I told myself, "They are good friends to me, Mr. Brown and Mr. Hamilton!"

I got my free papers that afternoon, and we went on with our journey, which took three days. At last, we arrived in the great city of Washington. We had twenty-four hours before we needed to meet the other circus people. So we walked through the busy streets, looked at the many interesting places in the city, and enjoyed watching the people in their beautiful clothes.

That evening, during dinner in the hotel, my friends were drinking more than usual. They gave me one glass of wine, too, but soon after I drank it, I began to feel very sick. My head and stomach hurt badly, and Brown and Hamilton had to help me upstairs to bed. I was in great pain, and could not sleep all night.

*Brown and Hamilton had to help me upstairs to bed.*

I do not know how long I was sick – perhaps only that night, or perhaps many days and nights. I cannot remember what happened next. I only know that I went to sleep at last, and when I woke up, I was lying on the ground in a small room, with heavy chains on my hands and feet. It was dark, and I could see nothing. My head still felt very strange, and at first, I could not think.

"Where am I?" I asked myself. "Where are Mr. Brown and Mr. Hamilton? How did I get here?" I felt in my pockets; my money and papers were not there! "There has been a mistake," I said to myself at first. "I'm a free man from New York. No one can put me here like this!"

But then a terrible idea came into my head: "Perhaps someone has kidnapped me!" Deep inside me, I knew that it was true. And I put my head in my hands and cried.

## Chapter Two
# THE SLAVE-HOUSE

Some hours later, I heard a key in a lock, and the door of the room opened. A man came in. He was a large, strong-looking white man, with an angry face. His name, I learned later, was James Burch.

I looked around me, in the light from the door. The room was very small with no bed or chair, and it had a dirty floor and stone walls.

"Well, my boy," said Burch, "how do you feel now?"

"I feel very sick," I replied. "Why am I here?"

"You're my slave," he said with a cruel smile. "I've bought you, and I'm going to send you south to Louisiana, to work on the farms there."

"But I'm a free man!" I shouted. "My name is Northup, and I live in Saratoga, in New York State! Take off my chains at once! I want to go home."

"Don't talk like that, boy," Burch said. "You're from Georgia, and you're a slave."

"I'm a free man!" I said again. "You can't do this!" Again and again, I said that I was no man's slave, and I told him to take off my chains. But suddenly he became angry.

"Shut your mouth, you black liar!" he shouted. "Be quiet, I say! You're my slave, not a free man!"

Behind the door, there was a big heavy stick. Suddenly,

*"Shut your mouth, you black liar!"*

Burch took it and began to hit me hard. Because my hands and feet were in chains, I could do nothing. I lay on the floor, while the heavy stick hit my back again and again.

When Burch's arm was tired, he stopped.

"Tell me, do you still think that you're a free man?" he asked. He was holding the stick above me.

"Yes, yes!" I replied, and he hit me once more. Again and again, he asked me the same question, and again and again, I answered with the same words.

The blood was running down my back, but Burch went on hitting me. At last, when I could not speak anymore, he stopped.

"Never say again that you are a free man," he said through his teeth, "or I will kill you!"

He left the room, and locked the door behind him. I lay shaking on the ground. My back was on fire, and I could not move.

I spent three or four days and nights in that dark room. Twice a day, Burch put meat, bread, and water just inside the door. I tried to eat, but I could not. I was in terrible pain, and it was difficult for me to move. When I thought about my family, I cried and cried.

But I still had hope, at that time. I still thought that I would soon be free. "Mr. Brown and Mr. Hamilton will find me," I told myself. "And when they explain that I'm not a slave, I'll be free again."

It was a great surprise to me when at last the door of my room opened and Burch pushed me outside. There I saw other slaves. This, I could see now, was a slave-house, and Burch kept his slaves here before he took them to the slave states in the south. High walls went all around the house, so nobody could see in from the street.

Burch gave me an old blanket – and for the next twelve years, I slept with nothing more than that. I stayed in Burch's slave-house for about two weeks, and, when he was not listening, I soon began to talk to the other slaves and hear their stories.

One night, he brought into my room a young woman named Eliza. She had two children: a boy named Randall, who was ten, and a daughter named Emily, who was only seven years old. Eliza held them in her arms and cried desperately over them.

"Oh, my dear children, they're going to take you from me, I know!" she cried. "What can I do? How can I live without you?" Again and again, she screamed wildly and fell on the floor, crying.

The next night, the door opened and Burch came in. "Wake up, all of you!" he said. "You're going south on the boat tonight!"

I helped Eliza with the children, and carried our blankets. Burch's men pushed us out of the building with the other slaves.

It was a dark night, and no one was in the streets. I

wanted to try to escape – but we were all in chains, and I could do nothing. So we walked silently through the quiet streets of Washington.

A boat was waiting for us at the river, and Burch and his men shut us in the hold – the place that was usually for boxes and animals and things. Soon, we began to move down the river. None of us slept that night, and many of the slaves were crying. I tried to be strong, and in my head, I made a hundred plans for escape.

*We walked silently through the quiet streets of Washington.*

The next day, we got off the boat, and Burch and his men drove us to a town called Richmond. There, they put us on a ship, and then left us and went back to Washington.

He was a slave-trader, James Burch – buying and selling slaves was his business. He knew that he was doing something dangerous when he sold me, a free man, into slavery. Before he left, he looked me hard in the eye, and said, "Just remember: if you talk about New York to anyone, or say that you're a free man, I will kill you."

Our ship was taking us by sea to New Orleans, the largest city in the slave state of Louisiana. It was a terrible journey. Soon after we left Richmond, we came through a great storm. "We are going to die," I thought to myself. Two of the other slaves and I decided to steal the ship's small boat and try to escape. But just when our plans were ready, one of the other two slaves became sick, and a few days later, he was dead. His death hit us badly, and without him, we could not escape. So our plans came to nothing.

When we arrived in New Orleans, Louisiana, I knew that there was no hope for me. No one was coming to help me. I started to think about Brown and Hamilton then. Did *they* kidnap me, and was the circus all a story? I did not know, and still do not know. I knew only one thing at that time: I wanted to be dead, like that poor slave on the ship.

## Chapter Three
# LOUISIANA

In New Orleans, a tall man with a thin face came on to the ship. His name was Theophilus Freeman.

"Where are Burch's slaves?" he asked the ship's men. "Over there? Right!" He took a paper from his pocket and read out names from it. "Eliza, Emily, Randall…" Each person came to stand near him, and at last, I was the only person waiting for my name. "Platt," he called out. No one moved.

"You!" Freeman shouted angrily at me. "Your name's Platt! Why don't you come here?"

"Platt is not my name," I replied politely.

"Well, that's what Burch calls you, so now you're Platt. Come here!"

Freeman took us to his slave-house, and told us to wash and put on new clothes. Then he and his men pushed us all into a very large room, which was called the "show-room." There were about fifty of us in that room – men, women, and children, all black. We had to stand there silently, like animals.

Many white men began to arrive, and I soon understood what was happening. This was a slave market, and the men were there to buy us. They looked very carefully at us. Sometimes they felt our arms to see how strong we were. Sometimes they looked at our teeth or eyes, and sometimes they told us to walk around while they watched us.

One man decided to buy Eliza's son, Randall. Eliza fell to the ground in front of him and cried wildly, "Take me and my daughter, too, master! Keep us together! Please, master!"

*"Keep us together! Please, master!"*

Freeman was very angry with Eliza. "I'll whip you if you scream like that again!" he shouted at her. But nothing could quiet the poor mother. Again and again, she asked the man desperately to take her and Emily, too. But the man only had money for one child slave. When he turned to leave with Randall, Eliza ran to the boy and took him in her arms, crying.

"Don't cry, Mama, I'll be a good boy!" said Randall. It was terrible to watch.

No one bought Eliza or me that day. But two weeks later, a tall man came into the show-room. He was about forty, with a kind face and a quiet voice. He did not look at our eyes, teeth, hands, or legs. He asked us questions and listened to our answers.

"Well, Mr. Freeman," he said at last, "I'll give you a thousand dollars for this one. Platt's his name, isn't it? And seven hundred for the young woman named Eliza. They'll work well, I think, and they'll be happy with me."

Poor Eliza screamed loudly, "No, no, I can't leave my little Emily!" She held her small daughter in her arms.

Freeman shouted at her, and then he hit her. She nearly fell, but went on crying desperately, "I've lost my son! Leave me one of my children! Master, dear master, please buy her too! I'll die if you take me from her!"

Our new master was sorry for her. "Mr. Freeman, how much do you want for the little girl?" he asked.

"That beautiful little thing? I'm not selling *her*!" replied Freeman, laughing. "She'll earn a lot more money for me when she's older! No, I'm keeping her!"

He pulled Eliza, still crying, from her daughter.

"Don't leave me, Mama!" cried little Emily.

But we could do nothing, and our new master took Eliza and me quickly out into the street. For a long time, we could still hear Emily's screams.

Eliza never saw Emily or Randall again. But she never stopped talking about them and thinking about them, and she cried for her children every day of her short life.

———◆———

Our new master was called William Ford, and he had a large farm on the Red River, in the middle of Louisiana. During the journey there, I wanted to explain to Ford that I was a free man. But I was afraid. "Mr. Ford's a good man," I said to myself. "He won't want to do anything that's against the law. If he knows that I'm a free man, perhaps he will sell me to another master – a much worse one." I thought about it many times, but at last, I decided to say nothing to anyone about my life in Saratoga.

Ford's farmhouse was very big, with woods all around it, and fruit trees in the garden. When we arrived, Ford sent Eliza and me to the slave cabin at the back of the house. Here we met the other slaves, and Ford's cook. She gave us a good meal of cornbread and bacon, and told us to rest after our long journey.

When I lay down to sleep that night, I could not stop thinking. I thought about how I would ever escape from this place, and I asked myself again and again, "How did this happen to me?" But more than anything, I thought of my family, at home in Saratoga.

The next day, our work began. Ford was kind to Eliza, who was still crying desperately for her children. He did not send her into the fields, but told her to work in the house for Mrs. Ford. That would be easier for her, he said.

The farm on Red River was not Ford's only farm. He had a large timber plantation four miles away at a place called Indian Creek, and his wife also had a big farm, with many slaves, at Bayou Boeuf. Every day that summer, I worked on the timber plantation with the other men. We had to cut the wood, carry it, and put it on wagons. There was a lot to do, and it was heavy work.

Ford kept slaves, but he was not like Burch or Freeman. Because his father and grandfather always had slaves, he did not think that it was wrong to buy and sell people. But there was never a kinder man than him. We were lucky to have him as our master, and we all knew it. Because Ford was kind to us, we all worked hard for him. Other masters needed to whip their slaves, but not Ford.

Because I liked to please Ford, I thought of an idea to help him. Ford had to send his timber to a place called Lamourie, and he used expensive drivers and wagons to do this. There was a river that went from Ford's plantation at Indian Creek to Lamourie, and I wanted to take the timber on the river. When I asked Ford about it, he said that I could try. So the next day, I made a raft, put some timber on it, and three slaves and I used long sticks to push it through the water.

We brought the wood to Lamourie without any accident, and when we arrived, everyone was jumping up and down excitedly at the side of the river. Ford thanked me warmly. From that day, I took all of Ford's timber to Lamourie on my rafts. People began to call me "the cleverest slave on the Red River."

*We brought the wood to Lamourie without any accident.*

Chapter Four
# A NEW MASTER

One day, a white man came to do some work on Ford's farmhouse at Indian Creek. His name was John Tibeats. He had no home, but moved from one farm to another, looking for work. He was the opposite of Ford in every way. He was a cruel, angry little man, and he was quick to shout at anyone who did not please him. There was no one, black or white, who liked him.

By the winter of 1842, Ford had some money trouble, and he had to sell some slaves. He decided to sell me to Tibeats. That was an unlucky day for me. I had to say goodbye to my friends, leave Ford, and begin a new life with my second master, Tibeats.

My first job for Tibeats was at Mrs. Ford's farm near the Bayou Boeuf River, twenty-seven miles away from Ford's house. Tibeats had to do some work there, so he took me with him. The Bayou Boeuf was a big, slow river, with cotton and sugar plantations on each side – and all around it, there were dangerous swamps full of alligators.

Eliza was working on the farm. It was good to see her again, but she looked thin and ill, and was still heavy with the pain of losing her children. "Do you remember little Emily and Randall?" she asked me again and again. I could only listen to her, and put an arm around her.

The farm manager at Bayou Boeuf was a kind man named Chapin. Like most people, he did not like Tibeats, but he knew that I was a good worker.

I had to work very hard for Tibeats. But he never said a kind word to me, and he shouted at me from morning until night.

My first fight with Tibeats came when we were building a small cabin near the Bayou Boeuf farmhouse. One evening, Tibeats told me to get up early the next day, to ask Chapin for some nails, and to start nailing wood to the outside of the cabin.

I was hard at work when he arrived the next morning, but he looked even angrier than usual.

"I told you to start nailing the wood!" he said.

"Yes, master," I replied quietly, "and I'm doing it, on the other side of the building, master."

He went to the other side and looked at my work.

"Didn't I tell you to get the nails from Chapin?" he shouted, when he came back.

"Yes, master, and I did—"

"Those nails are no good!" he shouted. "You black liar!" He ran to the farmhouse, and brought back with him one of the manager's largest and heaviest whips. He walked up to me and shouted angrily, "I'm going to teach you a lesson, Platt! Take your clothes off, you scoundrel!"

"Master Tibeats," I replied, looking him in the face, "I will not."

*"I'm going to teach you a lesson, Platt!"*

He jumped on me, with the whip above his head. But I was quicker than him. Before he could hit me, I pulled him down on the ground and put my foot on his neck. I was very angry, and the blood ran through my body like fire. I took the whip from his hand, and hit him again and again with it.

"Murder! Murder! Stop!" he screamed.

But, just like Tibeats himself, who never stopped whipping his slaves when they screamed, I did not stop now. I went on whipping him, and I only stopped when Chapin arrived on his horse. Slowly, Tibeats stood up and looked at me, with an angry face.

"What is this, Platt?" Chapin asked, from his horse.

"Master wanted to whip me because I used those nails," I answered.

"What's wrong with the nails, Mr. Tibeats?" Chapin asked.

"They're too big," Tibeats said, and his eyes did not leave me for a second.

"*I* gave Platt those nails," said Chapin. "This is Mrs. Ford's farm, and *I* am manager here. Do you understand that, Mr. Tibeats?"

Tibeats said nothing, but turned away from us. He got on his horse and rode away, down the road.

"Stay here, Platt," said Chapin, and he went back to the farmhouse.

"What have I done?" I thought, and I put my head in my hands and cried. "I've whipped my master, a white man! Now they'll kill me!"

An hour later, Tibeats came back. There were two white men with him, and they were carrying whips and a long rope.

"Stand still, you black good-for-nothing!" cried Tibeats.

I knew that I could not fight, or run away. I stood quietly while the men tied my hands and feet together, and then put the rope around my neck.

"Now," said one of the men, "where shall we hang the scoundrel?"

All hope died for me then. I thought that I would never see my wife and children again. But suddenly, Chapin walked out of the farmhouse. He had a gun in each hand.

"Stop right there!" he shouted. "Anyone who touches that slave again is a dead man. Mr. Tibeats, it's *you* who is the scoundrel here! I never knew a better worker than Platt. I told you already, this is Mrs. Ford's farm, and while Mr. Ford is away, *I'm* the master here. Now get away from here, all three of you!"

The two men hurried to their horses and rode away, and a few minutes later, Tibeats went, too.

Chapin did not cut the ropes around my neck, hands, and feet. Perhaps he was afraid, because I was Tibeats' slave – or perhaps he wanted Ford to see Tibeats' cruelty. He sent a slave to Ford's farmhouse on the Red River, and I had to stay outside in the hot sun, until at last Ford arrived on his horse. I was so happy to see him! He cut the ropes and sent me to the slave cabin for a rest. That evening, after Tibeats came back, we all heard a long and angry conversation between him and Ford up at the farmhouse.

The next day, Tibeats said nothing to me, and I went on working for him as usual. But I knew that Tibeats would not forget our fight, and after that, I was afraid for my life. Every day, I had one eye on my work and one eye on my master.

"Stop right there!" Chapin shouted.

One morning, about a month later, Chapin left the plantation for the day. I was working on the walls of a new cabin when Tibeats came and stood looking hard at me. Suddenly he shouted, "You've done that wrong, you black good-for-nothing!" I knew that my work was good, so I said carefully, "We always do it like this, master."

"You black liar!" he shouted, and then he took a big knife, and ran at me. "I'll cut your head open!" he cried.

It was life or death. There was only one thing to do. I caught his arm, and held him by the neck. In his eyes, I could see murder. I hit him, and he fell to the ground. Then I took the knife from him. He was like a wild animal. He saw a big stick on the ground, and he got up quickly and ran at me with the stick in his hand. I was stronger than him, so I pulled it from him. Again, I held him by the neck, this time with both hands. His face began to lose all color, and he looked terribly afraid.

A voice in my head said, *You only need to hold his neck a little longer, and he will die.* But I was afraid to kill him – and I was afraid to leave him alive, too. So I decided to run.

I dropped Tibeats on the ground, and left him there. Then I ran across the plantation, and into the trees. I waited there for some minutes, shaking. When I looked back, I saw Tibeats on his horse with some other men and a group of dogs. They were coming for me.

## Chapter Five
# IN THE SWAMPS

I went on running away from the plantation, and soon I was in the swamps. I could hear the dogs behind me, getting nearer and nearer. I knew those dogs. White men used them on all the Bayou Boeuf plantations to catch slaves who tried to escape. The dogs could run very fast, and when they got their teeth into your legs, you could not shake them off. Everyone was afraid of them.

I never knew a slave who escaped alive from Bayou Boeuf. Most slaves do not know how to swim, and you cannot go far in the swamps before you arrive at a river. So when a slave tried to escape, either the dogs got them, or they jumped into the waters and died.

Luckily for me, I am a good swimmer. When there was water under my feet, I began to feel better. "If I can get into the river," I thought, "the dogs won't smell me, and perhaps I can escape from them!"

I ran faster and faster, and at last I came to a big river and jumped in. I knew that the waters here were full of snakes and alligators, but I thought only of the dogs. I ran and swam through the river as fast as I could.

I went on and on through the water, and after a while, the sound of the dogs became quieter. I was losing them. By early afternoon, I could hear nothing of them. I could go more slowly now, but I began to think of the other dangers around me. The water snakes were everywhere. They usually moved away when I came nearer, but sometimes I nearly put my hand or foot on one, and I knew that they could easily kill a man. I also saw many alligators, big and small, on the ground near the river. I was terribly afraid of them, too.

*The waters here were full of snakes and alligators.*

Night came, and all was dark around me. I was afraid of everything that moved. I knew that I could not go on through the swamps – but I could not go back either. I did not want anyone to find me and take me back to Tibeats.

At last, I decided to travel northwest, to Ford's farm. "I will not be in danger there," I thought. Hour after hour, I walked through the swamps. I was dirty, hungry, and tired, and there were cuts all over my face, hands, and legs. But at last, there was no more deep water, and the ground became harder and harder. I was coming to the end of the swamps.

In the early light of the morning, I arrived at an opening in the trees, and saw a white man. I was afraid. Slaves needed papers to travel alone, and there was terrible trouble for those who went out without them. But I did not have any. So I decided to ask the white man a question quickly, before he could ask *me* anything.

"Can you tell me the way to William Ford's house?" I said. I was shaking, but I tried not to show it.

The man was surprised, and perhaps a little afraid of me. "You'll find the road to Ford's over there," he said.

I hurried away, before the man could ask me who I was. It was a lucky escape.

At about eight o'clock that morning, I arrived at Ford's farmhouse. I looked terrible, and when Mrs. Ford opened the door, she did not know who I was at first.

She went to get Ford, and I told him about my second fight with Tibeats, and my escape through the swamps. He listened carefully, and when I finished, he said kindly, "Go to the slave cabin and have a good meal. Then go to bed. You need to rest."

That meal was my first food in twenty-four hours. I was hungry and tired, but the sound of Ford's kind voice was better than food or sleep to me. I was not afraid anymore. When I went to bed, I slept deeply. The sleep took all my worries from me, and I saw again the sweet faces of my children, far away in Saratoga.

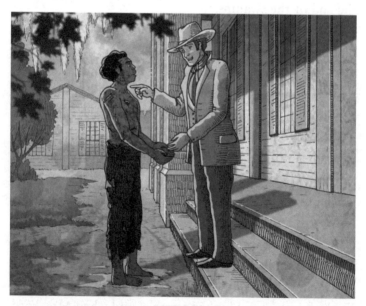

*Ford's kind voice was better than food or sleep to me.*

## Chapter Six
# A SLAVE'S LIFE

During the next few days, I rested, and ate, and worked for Mrs. Ford in her garden. Then Ford decided to take me back to Bayou Boeuf. I was sorry to leave. I loved Ford's place, because I never felt in danger there.

When we were on the road to Bayou Boeuf, a man rode up to us. It was Tibeats! He turned his horse and rode beside Ford, and I listened to their conversation.

"So Platt is still alive!" said Tibeats. "He's a good runner, that boy is! And a good swimmer, too!"

"Yes, and he's always been a good worker for me," replied Ford. "You need to be kinder to your slaves, Mr. Tibeats. You'll have to sell him now or send him to work in another place. You and he can't live together."

When we arrived at Bayou Boeuf, I was happy to see all my friends in the slave cabin again. But I was not there for long. Tibeats was a cruel man, but he did listen to Ford, and he sent me to work on another man's plantation for a while. I stayed there for four weeks, and went back to Bayou Boeuf one weekend to visit Eliza and the other slaves.

Poor Eliza looked thin and old. The pain of losing her children was too much for her. She could not work anymore – she was too sick.

*I went back to Bayou Boeuf one weekend.*

The day after my visit to Bayou Boeuf, Tibeats sold
me to a new master, Edwin Epps, and I left Mrs. Ford's
farm for the last time. Eliza died only a few months after
that, I heard later – free at last from the terrible pain of
her life.

And so I went to work on Edwin Epps's cotton farm
near Marksville, by the Red River – my home for the
next ten years of my life. Epps was a big, heavy man
with cold blue eyes. He was not a thinking man, like
Ford. He was a drinker, and everyone on the Red River
knew how cruel he was. When he was drunk, he shouted
terribly, and used his heaviest whip on his slaves.

Life on the cotton farm was very hard. We had to plant cotton in March and April, then work the ground next to the young cotton plants every two weeks. Cotton plants come up from the ground in only a week, and in a few months, they become as tall as a man.

By late August, the cotton was ready for picking and the fields looked like they were dressed with snow. This was the first of four picking times in the year. At picking time, every slave was out in the fields in the hot sun. We all put cotton in our bags as fast as we could, and when the bags were full, we put the cotton into large boxes.

At the end of the day, the farm manager weighed the boxes. If we did not pick as much as usual, Epps was always ready with his whip.

*At the end of the day, the farm manager weighed the boxes.*

"How much has Platt picked?" Epps shouted most days. "Not as much as yesterday? I knew it! Come here, boy!" And I felt the whip hit my back, again and again.

The work was hard, and it was a long day, from first light to night-time. We could only rest for fifteen minutes in the middle of the day, when we ate our lunch, a very small piece of cold bacon and cornbread.

The end of the day in the cotton fields was not the end of our work. After the manager weighed the cotton, and after the whippings, we had to give food to Epps's animals, cut our firewood, make a fire, and cook our evening meal. There was no tea, coffee, sugar, or salt. Each slave only had a little corn, which they used to make bread. The manager gave each of us a little bacon every week, and we cooked some of this over the fire, late at night. Sometimes the bacon was bad, but there was no other food to eat, so we were often hungry.

At last, at about midnight, we lay down on the floor. There was no bed – we each slept on a piece of wood, with an old blanket. We were very tired, but we were always afraid to sleep too deeply. We had to get up an hour before daylight, and there were terrible whippings for anyone who slept too late.

On Epps's farm, the days were sometimes even longer than this. When he was drunk, he called us into the farmhouse, and I had to play my violin while the other slaves danced. "Dance, you blacks! Dance!" he shouted again and again. We were desperately tired after our day's work, but when we stopped dancing, Epps broke chairs against the walls, shouted angrily, and whipped us. So we danced until we were half dead.

*We danced until we were half dead.*

There were terrible whippings at all times of the year. If the manager found a dry leaf in the cotton, he whipped his slave twenty-five times. If he thought that a slave was lazy in the field, he whipped them a hundred times. And if a poor slave tried to escape, he whipped them five hundred times.

We slaves were always afraid – afraid of waking up late, afraid of picking cotton too slowly, afraid of picking a leaf, afraid of standing still.

The only happy time for slaves during the year was at Christmas. Then, hundreds of slaves, wearing their best clothes, came together on one of the farms for a Christmas supper. We had a wonderful meal of meat, vegetables, fruit, and sweets – so different from our usual cornbread and bacon! There was music and dancing in the starlight, and then we had a few days without any work. Our master gave us papers, and we could then visit other places near the plantation freely. Christmas was the only truly happy time in a slave's life.

I often played my violin at Christmas dances. My violin was my greatest friend during those long years in slavery. Because people often asked me to play at their big houses, it took me away from the fields for a while, and it earned me a little money to buy some food or some new shoes. But, more importantly, its music quieted the pain of my life as a slave. When I played, I could forget the cruelty of my master for a short time.

Ten years I worked for that man Epps, with no thanks. And for ten years, he called me bad names and gave me whippings. He forgot that his black slaves were people. He thought that they belonged to him and were no better than his dogs.

*Christmas was the only truly happy time in a slave's life.*

## Chapter Seven
# ESCAPE PLANS

Two years after I arrived at the cotton farm, Epps bought a plantation near the Bayou Boeuf, and took some of his slaves there with him. But that year, most of the cotton plants died, and there was no work for us. So Epps sent some of us to work for another farmer on a large sugar-cane plantation.

I was much better at cutting sugar cane than picking cotton, and I earned some money on the sugar plantation, too. Sunday was usually a free day for us slaves, but during cane-cutting time, we all had to work seven days a week, and our master paid us for our Sundays. We had nothing that belonged to us, only our sleeping-blankets, so most of us spent the money on something useful like a knife or cooking pot.

When we went back to Epps's farm near the Bayou Boeuf, he decided to make me a slave-driver in the cotton fields. My job was to carry a whip and use it on any slave who did not work hard. I did not want to hurt any of my friends. So, when I had to whip someone, I held the whip high, then stopped it just before it touched a slave's back. The slave understood this, and was ready to scream loudly. Epps watched me carefully, but he never knew that I was not really whipping anyone.

*I stopped the whip just before it touched a slave's back.*

I was Epps's slave-driver for eight years, and I know that life was a little easier for slaves who worked under me.

———————

Slaves often tried to escape, and many of them lost their lives. There was a young slave boy on a farm next to Epps's who ran away one day after a terrible whipping, and hid in the sugar cane. The manager sent his dogs after the boy, and when they caught him, they bit great pieces from his body. The poor boy died, in great pain, soon after.

During all these long years of my slavery, I never stopped thinking of ways to escape. Once, when Epps sent me to a farm near the big River Teche for a while, I spoke to someone who worked on a ship. He was going north, and I asked him to take me with him secretly. He wanted to help me, but it was too dangerous for him, and he explained sadly to me that it was not possible.

My great hope was to write a letter to my friends in the north, and ask them to rescue me. But no slave has a pen or paper, and no mail office will send a letter for a slave. Writing a letter was dangerous, too. Epps heard when he bought me that I could read and write, and he told me then, "If I ever see you with a book, or a pen and paper, I will give you the biggest whipping of your life."

But one day, when Epps was away, Mrs. Epps sent me to the nearest town to buy some things for her – and one of those things was some paper. On the way home, I took one piece of the paper, and hid it in my cabin.

The next few nights, I worked hard to make a pen from things that lay around the plantation. At last, one night, while everyone was asleep, I wrote a long letter to one of my friends in Saratoga, asking for help. Then I hid the letter under my blanket in the slave cabin.

It stayed there for a long time, but then one day, a man named Armsby came to work for Epps. He was white, so he could come and go at the farm, and he worked with us slaves in the cotton fields. I did not like him much, but he was my only hope. So one day, I asked him to post the letter for me and gave him some money.

"Please don't tell Master Epps about this!" I said to him. "If you do, he'll whip me to death!"

*One night, I wrote a long letter to one of my friends.*

"No, no, I won't tell him," he replied, taking the money. "Just bring me the letter tomorrow."

But I was not sure about Armsby, and I did not take the letter to him at once. I was right to wait. Two days later, I saw him with Epps, and they were talking quietly together. That night, Epps came into the slave cabin with a whip in his hand.

"Well, boy," he said to me, "I hear that I have a slave who writes letters and asks white men to post them!"

"I don't know anything about that," I said.

"You asked that man Armsby to post a letter for you!" he went on.

I had to think quickly. "I know nothing about it, master," I said. "I have no pen or paper to write a letter. That Armsby is a liar, everybody knows that."

I told Epps not to listen to Armsby. I said that I was a good slave, and that Armsby was lying because he wanted Epps to give him more work.

At last Epps looked at me and said, "So Armsby thinks that he knows my slaves better than me, does he? I'll show him!"

He left the cabin, and I put my letter on the fire, and watched unhappily while it burned to nothing. We did not see Armsby again after that.

I went on thinking of ways to escape. Every day during my ten years with Epps, I had a new plan. Hope of rescue was the only thing that kept me alive.

## Chapter Eight
# PATSEY

Edwin Epps thought that he could break any man or woman with his whip. Our backs, legs, and arms all carried cuts from his cruelty. But the worst whipping in my time as a slave happened to Patsey. She was the best cotton-picker on Epps's farm.

Patsey was a beautiful black girl, twenty-three years old, and strong and fast. When I first met her, she was always laughing. She could drive horses, cut wood, and work harder than most men. But on her back were the cuts from thousands of whippings – because Epps liked to talk and laugh with Patsey, and his wife saw that. Epps whipped her if she did not spend time with him, and Mrs. Epps whipped her if she did. Mrs. Epps told her husband to send Patsey away, but Epps did not want to sell her. So Mrs. Epps did everything possible to hurt poor Patsey: more than once, she even asked me to secretly kill her.

One Sunday, when we were washing our clothes in the river, Epps could not find Patsey. She was away for two hours, and when she came back, he was very angry.

"Where have you been, girl?" he shouted at her.

"I've been to see Mrs. Shaw at the Shaws' farm," replied Patsey. "She's kind to me."

"You black liar!" shouted Epps. "You go to the Shaws' farm to visit Mr. Shaw himself! That's it, isn't it?"

*"You black liar!" shouted Epps.*

"No, master, I'm no liar!" cried Patsey.

But Epps was not listening. "I'll teach you a lesson, girl!" he shouted. "Lie down! Platt, push four big sticks into the ground, then tie her hands and feet to them."

He brought his heaviest whip from the house, and gave it to me. "Now, Platt, let's see how strong you are. Go on, whip her!" he shouted.

I tried not to whip Patsey too hard, but blood soon began to run down her back.

"Hit her harder!" Epps shouted. "Or I'll whip you next!"

I hit her thirty or forty times, but at last I dropped the whip. "I won't do it anymore, master!" I cried.

Epps took the whip himself then, and hit her much, much harder. All the time, she was screaming, and he was shouting. But at last, her screams stopped. I thought that she was dying!

The birds were singing and the sun was warm, but this was a truly terrible hour. I heard the sound of the whip on Patsey's back, again and again, and I thought to myself, "There can be nothing worse than this, at this minute, in any corner of the world."

In the end, Epps stopped, and we carried poor Patsey to the slave cabin. We washed her back with salt and water, and sat with her while she cried. Day after day, she lay there in the cabin, in terrible pain, and it was a long time before she could move again.

She was a different person when at last she came back to the cotton fields. She never smiled or laughed again, and she worked without a word. The pain of that terrible whipping broke her for life.

## Chapter Nine
# A TRUE FRIEND

In June 1852, a white worker arrived to build a new house for Epps. His name was Bass, and he was a kind, hard-working man. He always spoke freely and said what he was thinking, and everyone at Bayou Boeuf liked him.

One day, he and Epps were talking, and I heard their conversation. It was very interesting to me, because it was about slavery.

"I tell you, Mr. Epps," Bass said, "slavery is all wrong. Why do you have slaves to work for you?"

"Because I paid good money for them!" laughed Epps. "And the law says that they belong to me!"

"I'm sorry, but the law is a liar," replied Bass. "You don't buy white men, do you? And a white man and a black one are just the same."

"Of course they aren't! Blacks are no better than animals. Everyone knows that. You just like to talk too much, Mr. Bass!" Epps laughed again while they walked away.

I thought about this for a long time, and I decided to talk to Bass. I knew that I needed to be careful, but one day, when I was working alone with him, I started a conversation.

"Where do you come from, master?" I asked.

"You won't know the place, Platt," he replied with a smile. "I come from Canada."

"Oh, I've been there," I answered. "When I was younger, I worked in Montreal and Kingston."

Bass looked at me in great surprise. "But you're a slave. What were you doing in Canada? And why are you here now?"

"I'm afraid to tell you, Master Bass," I said.

But he said that he would not tell anyone, and so, at last, I told him my story. It was a long one, but he listened carefully, and asked me a lot of questions.

When I finished my story, I asked him for help. "Will you write to my friends in Saratoga, and ask them to send free papers for me?" I said.

*At last, I told him my story.*

"Of course I will," said Bass. "But this is dangerous for both of us, so we must be very careful."

I gave him the name of my friend Mr. Parker, and of other friends who, I hoped, would help me. Then I thanked him warmly. I knew that he was a true friend now, and I told him about my wife and children.

"I want so much to hold them once more before I die!" I said.

Bass wrote the letters for me the next week, and I began my wait. Week after week, when Bass went to the mail office in the nearest town, Marksville, I asked him for news. But he always shook his head unhappily. I began to lose hope. "Perhaps the mail office has lost the letters," I thought. "Perhaps my friends in Saratoga have died, or forgotten me!"

The other slaves worried about me, because I was so quiet. "Are you sick, Platt?" Patsey asked me often. But I knew that no slave could help me, and that the secret of my life was dangerous for me and for them. So I said nothing.

At last, after about three months, Epps's new house was ready, and Bass had no more work there. Before he left, he spoke to me very quietly. "Don't worry, Platt – help will come. And if it doesn't, I'll travel all the way to Saratoga myself."

After Bass left, I could not talk to anyone about the letters. I just had to stay silent, and hope.

## Chapter Ten
# RESCUE

**C**hristmas came, and there was still no news. That winter was a very cold one, but we had to work out in the cotton fields every day.

One Monday morning – January 3rd, 1853 – it was even colder than usual. All of us slaves were picking cotton, when we saw two white men. They were walking through the fields.

When the men came near to us, one of them called out, "Which of you is Platt?"

"That's me, master," I replied.

"I'm the sheriff," he said. "Do you know this man?"

The second man came nearer, and I looked at him carefully. Who was he? A stranger? No! Suddenly I knew!

"Mr. Northup!" I shouted. It was Henry Northup, a lawyer from Sandy Hill, near Saratoga. He was a Northup from the family who first freed my father from slavery all those years ago.

He took both my hands and shook them warmly.

"Solomon," he said, "I'm so happy to see you. Put down that bag – this is the end of your cotton-picking days."

There was so much to say, but I could not speak. I stood there, crying, while I held on to his hands.

*I stood there, crying, while I held on to his hands.*

All the slaves watched in great surprise. This was my tenth year on Epps's farm, but they knew nothing of my real name or of my life in Saratoga.

At last, I found my voice, and asked Mr. Northup about my family. He said that my wife and children were all well, but that my mother was now dead. He took my arm, and we walked up to Epps's house with the sheriff. Epps was waiting for us, and when he saw Mr. Northup's papers, he was very angry.

"Who wrote and posted that letter for you, boy?" he shouted at me.

"Perhaps I wrote it myself," I replied.

"I'll kill the man who helped you, when I find him!" he shouted. But he could not stop me leaving. In the end, even Epps could not fight against the law.

When Mr. Northup, the sheriff, and I were going, Patsey ran up to say goodbye.

"Oh Platt," she cried, "you've helped me so much! Now you're going to be free, and I'm so happy for you! But what will happen to me?"

I did not know what to say. I looked back when we started to drive away. Patsey was standing there and watching with the other slaves. It was the last time I ever saw them. We turned a corner and they were gone.

Mr. Northup and I traveled back to Saratoga together. During our journey, he explained how he came to Louisiana to rescue me. Only one of Bass's letters ever arrived, he told me. It went to my friend Mr. Parker's house in Saratoga, and Mr. Parker took it to my wife immediately. My family then went to see Henry Northup, and at once, Mr. Northup began working on a plan to rescue me. He questioned my wife, talked to other lawyers, and visited many offices. When he had all the necessary papers, he made the long journey south to Louisiana, and came to find me with the sheriff from Marksville.

When I arrived at my house in Saratoga, I opened the door quietly. In a few seconds, my daughter Margaret was in my arms. She was married now, and had a young son! Then my other daughter Elizabeth and my wife Anne ran into the room. My son Alonzo was away working, they told me. But the rest of us were together at last. Soon, we were all laughing and crying and talking at the same time.

Words cannot begin to describe how we felt just then. But when we sat in front of the warm fire later that evening, we began to speak of our terrible pain, our worries, and our hopes during those years. They never stopped thinking of me, my family told me. And they never stopped hoping for my freedom.

My story has now ended. Every word of it is true. I am not the only free man who has known kidnap and slavery. Hundreds of free men and women are, I am sure, working right now on the plantations of Louisiana or Texas.

But I shall say no more about this. Twelve years of cruelty have quieted me. I want only to live a good life now, and, one day, to sleep next to my father's resting place.

# AFTERWORD

Solomon Northup wrote his book, *Twelve Years a Slave*, in 1853, after he became a free man once more. For the rest of his life, he worked hard to bring slavery to an end, and he traveled all over the northeast of the United States to give talks about his life as a slave. No one knows when, where, or how he died.

James Burch and the people who kidnapped Solomon Northup never went to prison for their crimes.

In 2013, a very famous film of Solomon's book was made by Steve McQueen. Suddenly everyone knew Solomon Northup's name. Now people can even walk the "Solomon Northup Trail," and visit the places in central Louisiana where Solomon lived and worked as a slave.

**alligator** *(n)* a big, long, and dangerous animal with many teeth, which lives in the water

**bacon** *(n)* long, thin pieces of meat

**become** *(v)* to begin to be something

**blanket** *(n)* a warm cover for a bed

**cabin** *(n)* a small, simple house made of wood

**chains** *(n)* "ropes" made of metal rings

**circus** *(n)* a show that moves from place to place, with people and animals who dance, jump, and do many clever things

**corn** *(n)* a plant that you can eat, which farmers grow in fields

**cotton** *(n)* We use cotton to make clothes and bedsheets, etc. It comes from a plant.

**cruel** *(adj)* very unkind; **cruelty** *(n)*

**desperately** *(adv)* having no hope; ready to do anything to get what you want

**drunk** *(adj)* when a person has drunk too much alcohol, e.g. wine or beer

**earn** *(v)* to get money for work

**farm** *(n)* People keep animals and grow food on a farm.

**hang** *(v)* to tie somebody up to something high, e.g. a tree, with a rope around the neck, because you want to kill them

**idea** *(n)* a new plan

**kidnap** *(v & n)* to take somebody away and hide them

**law** *(n)* A law says what people can or cannot do in a country.

**lawyer** *(n)* a person who has learned about law

**liar** *(n)* a person who says or writes things that are not true

**manager** *(n)* a person in a business, shop, farm, etc. who decides things and tells people what to do

**master** *(n)* a man who has people or animals that work for him

**nail** *(n & v)* a small, thin piece of metal which you hit into wood to hold things together

**pain** *(n)* what you feel in your body when you are hurt or sick

**pick** *(v)*  to take a flower, fruit, etc. from the ground or from a tree

**plant** *(n)*  a tree, flower, vegetable, etc. that grows from the ground; **plant** *(v)* to put things in the ground to grow

**plantation** *(n)*  a big piece of land to grow tea, sugar, cotton, etc.

**raft** *(n)*  a small boat with no sides and no engine

**rescue** *(v & n)*  to save somebody or something from danger

**rope** *(n)*  very thick, strong string to tie or pull things

**scoundrel** *(n)*  someone who lies and does bad things

**sheriff** *(n)*  a kind of policeman/woman in the USA

**slave** *(n)*  a person who belongs to another person and must work for them for no money

**slavery** *(n)*  being a slave; having slaves

**snake** *(n)*  an animal (often dangerous) with a long, thin body and no legs

**state** *(n)*  a part of a country

**sugar** *(n)*  something sweet from a plant; people put it in tea or coffee

**sugar cane** *(n)*  the plant that sugar comes from

**swamp** *(n)*  a place with soft, wet ground

**tie** *(v)*  to put rope, string, etc. around somebody or something

**timber** *(n)*  wood for building and making things

**violin** *(n)*  a musical instrument; to play it, you hold it next to your neck and move a special stick across the strings

**wagon** *(n)*  a moving vehicle with four wheels; horses pull it

**weigh** *(v)*  to use a machine to see how heavy somebody or something is

**whip** *(n & v)*  a long piece of leather or rope for hitting people or animals

**wine** *(n)*  an alcoholic drink

## American Slavery

Slavery in North America began after Britain took colonies there in the seventeenth century. Most of the slaves in North America came from Africa. People brought them to North America to work on big farms and plantations. The slaves belonged to the people who bought them, and had to work for no pay. During the American Revolution (1775–1783), the thirteen colonies of North America won their war against Britain. They were not colonies anymore: they became the United States of America. In some of these states, slavery was now against the law.

*Slaves working on a plantation in St. Louis*

## The abolition of slavery

In the first half of the nineteenth century, the abolitionist movement started. This was a large group of people who worked together for many years because they wanted the government to abolish slavery in the United States. There were artists, writers, and other famous people from all around the world in this group.

In 1861, the American Civil War started, largely because of slavery. People in the northern states wanted to abolish slavery across the country, but the south still needed thousands of slaves for the cotton and sugar-cane plantations. During the war, there was terrible fighting, and about 750,000 people died. But at last, in 1865, the the northern states won, and Abraham Lincoln's government abolished slavery.

*Abraham Lincoln visiting soldiers during the American Civil War*

**READ & RESEARCH** Read 'Beyond the Story' and research the answers to these questions.

1 Can you find the names of some famous abolitionists? How did they help to abolish slavery?

2 What was the underground railroad, and how did it help slaves?

**abolish** *(v)*  to stop or end something by law

**colony** *(n)*  a country or an area that is ruled by another country

**government** *(n)*  the group of people who rule or control a country

**soldier** *(n)*  a person in an army

## Think Ahead

1  Read about the story on the back cover. How much do you
know now about the story? Check (✓) the true sentences.

1  This is a true story.                          ☐

2  The story happens in Africa.                   ☐

3  Solomon steals something important.            ☐

4  People kidnap Solomon and sell him.            ☐

5  Solomon spends a long time away from home.  ☐

2  What is going to happen in the story? Can you guess?

1  Solomon works on farms and helps other slaves.

2  Solomon kills a white man and leaves the country.

3  Solomon is free in the end and goes back home.

3  **RESEARCH** Before you read, find the answers to these
questions.

1  This story begins in 1841. How many slaves were there
in the United States at that time?

2  Which of these states were slave states in 1841?

*Georgia   Louisiana   New York State   Washington*

# Chapter Check

**CHAPTER 1** Complete the sentences with the places below.
There is one extra name.

*Louisiana    New York City    New York State
Saratoga    Washington*

1  Solomon's family lives in a town called _____.

2  Their town is in _____.

3  Brown and Hamilton say that the circus is in

    _____.

4  Solomon gets his free papers in _____.

**CHAPTER 2** Are the sentences true or false?

1  Burch is going to send Solomon to work on farms.

2  Burch hides his slaves behind high walls.

3  Eliza has three children.

4  Solomon and two other slaves escape from the ship.

5  Burch travels with the slaves to New Orleans.

**CHAPTER 3** Put the events in order.

a  A man buys Eliza's son.

b  Solomon makes a raft.

c  Ford buys Solomon and Eliza.

d  Freeman takes the slaves to the slave market.

e  Solomon gets a new name.

**CHAPTER 4** Match the quotes with the people who say or think them in the chapter.

*Chapin   Eliza   Solomon   Tibeats   Tibeats' friend*

1  "Do you remember little Emily and Randall?"

2  "You black liar!"

3  "What have I done?"

4  "Where shall we hang the scoundrel?"

5  "It's *you* who is the scoundrel here!"

**CHAPTER 5** Correct the underlined words.

1  White men use <u>horses</u> to catch slaves who try to escape from plantations.

2  Most slaves cannot escape through the swamps because they do not know how to <u>fight</u>.

3  Solomon arrives at Ford's house in the <u>evening</u>.

4  After he has heard Solomon's story, Ford speaks <u>angrily</u> to him.

**CHAPTER 6** Answer the questions about a slave's life on a cotton farm.

1  What did slaves have to do in March and April?

2  What did slaves have to do in August?

3  When did slaves have to get up in the morning?

4  What did slaves have for lunch in the cotton field?

5  What did slaves sleep on at night?

**CHAPTER 7** Match the sentence halves.

1 Most of the cotton plants died, …

2 Solomon was better at cutting cane…

3 Solomon knew that life was a little easier for slaves…

4 The dogs once caught a young slave boy…

5 Solomon had to make a pen…

6 Armsby took Solomon's money…

a because he could not buy one.

b who tried to escape.

c than picking cotton.

d who worked under him in the field.

e so there was no work for the slaves.

f and told Epps about the letter.

**CHAPTER 8** Complete the sentences with the names of people in the story. You will need to use some of the names more than once.

*Epps   Mr. Shaw   Mrs. Shaw   Patsey   Solomon*

1 One Sunday, _____ went to visit her friend
   _____.

2 _____ became very angry with _____.

3 _____ thought that she was visiting
   _____.

4 _____ told _____ to tie _____ to
   sticks in the ground and whip her.

**CHAPTER 9** Choose the correct words to complete the sentences.

1 Bass is a *black / white* man.

2 Bass thinks that slavery is *right / wrong*.

3 Solomon's story *pleases / surprises* Bass very much.

4 Bass asks Solomon *a lot of / a few* questions.

5 Bass *finds / writes* some letters for Solomon.

6 Solomon has to wait a *long / short* time for news.

7 Patsey thinks that Solomon is *sick / afraid*.

**CHAPTER 10** Check (✓) the true sentences.

1 Mr. Henry Northup gets a letter from Solomon in the post.

2 Solomon's family asks Mr. Northup for help.

3 When Mr. Northup reads the letter, he travels to Louisiana at once.

4 The sheriff is a friend of Solomon's.

5 Solomon is picking cotton when Mr. Northup arrives.

6 Mr. Epps is happy that Solomon is now a free man.

7 Solomon tells Epps about Bass's help.

8 After he leaves Louisiana, Solomon never sees Patsey or the other slaves again.

9 Solomon finds his wife and three children at home when he arrives back.

## Focus on Vocabulary

**1 Complete the sentences with the correct words.**

*blanket   master   swamps   violin   wagons   weigh*

1 Solomon earns money when he plays his _____ for people.

2 The slaves sleep with nothing more than a _____.

3 William Ford is Solomon's first _____.

4 Farmers used _____ to carry timber over land.

5 The _____ near Ford's farm are full of wild animals.

6 Farm managers _____ the cotton at the end of the day.

**2 Replace the underlined words with the words below.**

*cabin   cruel   raft   rescue   scoundrel   sheriff*

1 Ford's slaves eat and sleep in a <u>small wooden house</u>.

2 Solomon builds a <u>wooden boat</u> for Ford.

3 Tibeats says that his slave is a <u>very bad man</u>.

4 Both Tibeats and Epps are <u>unkind</u>.

5 Bass helps to <u>save</u> Solomon from slavery.

6 Henry Northup and the <u>town policeman</u> come to Epps's farm to find Solomon.

## Focus on Language

1 **Complete the questions with the correct endings.**

You're going to whip me, _____ _____?
*You're going to whip me, aren't you?*

1 It's hard work, _____ _____?

2 You're working for Ford, _____ _____?

3 Tibeats is your master, _____ _____?

4 Randall was Eliza's son, _____ _____?

5 You've picked a lot of cotton, _____ _____?

6 You'll post my letter, _____ _____?

2 **DECODE** **Read this text from the story and underline all the personal pronouns (*I/me*, *we/us* etc).**

Mr. Northup took my arm, and we walked up to Epps's house with the sheriff. Epps was waiting for us, and when he saw Mr. Northup's papers, he was very angry.

"Who wrote and posted that letter for you?" he shouted at me.

"Perhaps I wrote it myself," I replied.

"I'll kill the man who helped you!" he shouted.

3 **DECODE** **Who does each pronoun stand for in exercise 1?**

## Discussion

1 **THINK CRITICALLY** Read the sentences. Do you agree with them? Why/Why not? Use the words below to discuss with a partner.

1 <u>I think that</u> Brown and Hamilton kidnapped Solomon.

2 <u>In my opinion,</u> Solomon made a mistake when he decided not to tell Ford he was a free man.

3 <u>I don't understand why</u> Ford thought that it was OK to have slaves.

*I agree/don't agree.    I think that's true.*
*You're right.    I don't think so.*

2 **COMMUNICATE** Talk about these questions with your partner. Use the <u>underlined</u> words in exercise 1.

1 What is the worst mistake that Solomon makes?

2 Which character in the story do you like best?

3 Which character are you most sorry for?

3 Choose a passage (a paragraph, or just one or two sentences) from the story. Complete the sentence below, and choose the best words.

I chose the passage that begins _____ on page _____ because it *surprised me / was funny / was very sad / was important.*

4 **COMMUNICATE** Take turns to read your passage to a partner and ask questions about it.

1  Read this profile of the slave Frederick Douglass.

**A** Frederick Douglass was born a slave in Maryland in 1818. He then went to live at the farm of Hugh Auld in Baltimore. When he was twelve years old, he began to learn to read with Auld's wife Sophia. Auld stopped the lessons, but Douglass went on learning from other white children who lived near the farm.

**B** In 1833, Douglass went to work for Edward Covey, a poor farmer who whipped his slaves. One time, Douglass fought back against Covey, and after that Covey did not whip him.

**C** Douglass tried to escape from slavery twice, with no luck. But in 1838, a free black woman called Anna Murray helped him. She gave him money, clothes, and a free man's papers, and he then escaped to New York.

**D** Douglass married Anna Murray that year, and they went to live in Massachusetts. They had five children.

**E** After 1838, Douglass gave lots of talks against slavery, and went to many abolitionist meetings. He worked on abolitionist newspapers and in politics. He also wrote a book called *Narrative of the Life of Frederick Douglass, an American Slave*.

**F** He died suddenly in 1895.

**2** Match the headings with the correct paragraphs.

*Death    Early Life    Escape    Family Life*
*Fighting His Master    Fighting Slavery*

**3** Read the text again and write questions for the answers.

1 In 1818.

2 Hugh Auld and Edward Covey.

3 A woman gave him money, clothes, and a free man's papers.

4 In 1838.

5 Yes, he was married to Anna Murray, and they had five children.

6 Yes, it was called *Narrative of the Life of Frederick Douglass, an American Slave.*

7 He gave talks against slavery, went to abolitionist meetings, and worked on abolitionist newspapers and in politics.

**4** CREATE Now answer the questions in exercise 3 about Solomon Northup, or about another famous slave. Use your answers, and other interesting information, to write a profile like the one about Frederick Douglass. Use the same headings.

## If you liked this Bookworm, why not try...

# Huckleberry Finn

**LEVEL 2**
Mark Twain
Retold by Diane Mowat

Who wants to live in a house, wear clean clothes, be good, and go to school every day? Not young Huckleberry Finn, that's for sure.

So Huck runs away, and is soon floating down the Mississippi River on a raft. With him is Jim, a black slave who is also running away. But life is not always easy for the two friends.

And there's 300 dollars waiting for anyone who catches poor Jim...

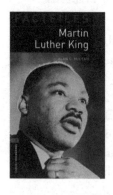

# Martin Luther King

**FACTFILES LEVEL 3**
Alan C. McLean

The United States in the 1950s and 60s was a troubled place. Black people were angry, because they did not have the same rights as whites. It was a time of angry words, of marches, of protests, a time of bombs and killings.

But above the angry noise came the voice of one man – a man of peace. "I have a dream," said Martin Luther King, and it was a dream of blacks and whites living together in peace and freedom. This is the story of an extraordinary man, who changed American history in his short life.